The Monkey Kingdom (Species of Monkeys): 3rd Grade Science Series

SPEEDY
PUBLISHING

Speedy Publishing LLC
40 E. Main St. #1156
Newark, DE 19711
www.speedypublishing.com

There are currently 264 known monkey species.

Pygmy marmosets are the smallest type of monkey. Pygmy marmosets do a lot of climbing because tree sap is their favorite food.

Mandrills mostly live in tropical rainforests. Mandrills have an omnivorous diet consisting mostly of fruits and insects.

The proboscis monkeys are native to the Borneo Island. Proboscis monkeys are omnivores and they primarily feed on leaves and fruits especially unripe fruits.

Japanese macaques are omnivores. Their diet consists of barks, twigs, fruit, insects, eggs and small mammals. Japanese macaques live in large groups called troops.

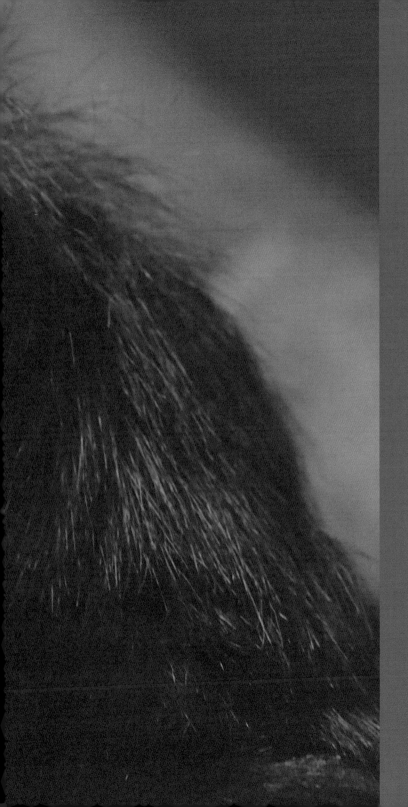

The White-faced Saki live in monogamous pairs or small family groups. The white-faced saki can be found in Brazil, French Guiana, Guyana, Suriname and Venezuela.

Howler monkeys are the loudest of all monkeys. These monkeys live in Central and South America.

The yellow baboon has a slim body with long arms and legs and a yellowish-brown hair. Yellow baboons use at least 10 different vocalizations to communicate.

Red-shanked douc is one of the most colourful primate species. the red-shanked douc spends almost all of its time feeding high in the treetops.

The pied tamarin is a small species of monkey found in the rainforest of Brazil. The pied tamarin is most active during the day and rests in the safety of the tree tops during the night.

The mona monkey lives throughout western Africa. Mona monkeys respond to danger by freezing in place.

The mantled guereza is native to much of west central and east Africa. The mantled guereza lives in social groups of three to fifteen individuals.

Gee's golden langur is considered sacred by many Himalayan people. The gee's golden langur can be found in a small region of western Assam, India.

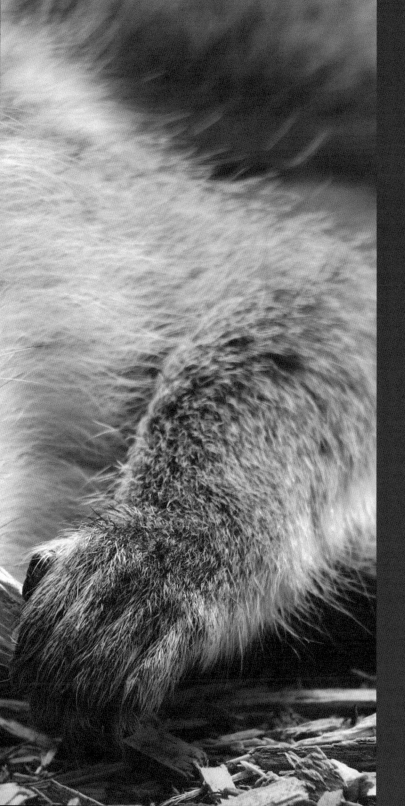

The grivet is most active in the morning and in early evening. Females will have a limited number of mates, while males will have numerous.

The Javan lutung is found on and endemic to the island of Java. It feeds mainly on leaves, fruit, flowers, flower buds, and insect larvae.

Printed in Great Britain
by Amazon